THANKS FOR
MY FORMAL
EDUCATION

(MUM AND DAD)

By
Stephen
Ezeagu

ISBN:
978-978-953-163-9

The Contents

DEDICATION

This book is
dedicated to God
Almighty

who made it
possible for me to
come up with this
wonderful book.

ACKNOWLEDGMENT

I am indebted to my wife, Chizzy Beauty, and my son Saviour

f o r   t h e i r
wonderful prayers
and support at all
times.

I also want to
acknowledge you
reading my book
right now.

God bless and
keep you all.

Chapter One
Ikpeama with
the Grandmother
in the Village

Chapter Two
Ikpeama moved
to the City

Chapter Three
Ikpeama in his Secondary School

Chapter Four

Ikpeama in the University

Chapter Five
Ikpeama
final year in the University

Questions

The book, Thanks for
my Formal Education
(Mum and Dad).

Is a wonderful story
book, which every
person who know the
value of education need
to read.

As parents, we need to
tell our children
exciting and educative
stories. True live story
or imagination story
can

change your child or
children attitude
toward thinking in a
right direction...

In the book, you will
get to know how story
telling changes a
person.

So, do the right thing
both parents and
children.